THE APE & THE WHALE

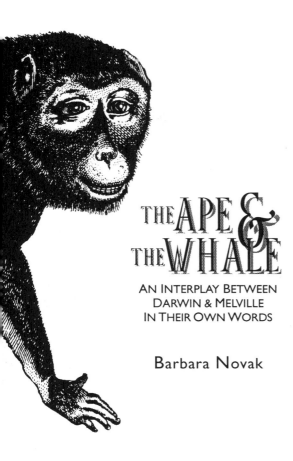

THE APE & THE WHALE

AN INTERPLAY BETWEEN DARWIN & MELVILLE IN THEIR OWN WORDS

Barbara Novak

HOMESTEAD PUBLISHING
Moose, Wyoming

ISBN 0-943972-33-7
Printed on recycled, acid-free paper

Library of Congress Cataloging-in-Publication Data

Novak, Barbara.
    The ape & the whale : an interplay between Darwin &
Melville in their own words / Barbara Novak. — 1st ed.
            p.   cm.
    ISBN 0-943972-33-7 : $12.95
    1. Melville, Herman, 1819-1891—Quotations. 2. Natural
history—Quotations, maxims, etc. 3. Darwin, Charles, 1809-
1882—Quotations. 4. Whales—Quotations, maxims, etc. 5.
Apes—Quotations, maxims, etc. I. Darwin, Charles, 1809-
1882. II. Melville, Herman, 1819-1891. III. Title. IV. Title:
Ape and the whale.
PS2382.N68   1995
813'.3—dc20   94-43742
                                                   CIP

Published by
HOMESTEAD PUBLISHING
Box 193, Moose, Wyoming 83012

First Edition

For Alan R. Novak

Preface

"Melville took an awful licking," Charles Olson wrote. "He was bound to. He was an original, aboriginal. A beginner." Charles Darwin was another kind of aboriginal, whose scientific discoveries ushered in the modern world of secular doubt and spiritual skepticism. The American and the Englishman wrote two of the greatest books of the nineteenth century: *Moby-Dick* and *The Origin of Species*. One achieved worldly success. The other had to await his apotheosis in Paradise, with his "celestial legs" crossed "in the celestial grass that is forever tropical."

Almost ten years separated them in life and in death. Darwin was born on February 12th, 1809 in Shrewsbury, England, Herman Melville on August 1st, 1819 in New York City. Both died in their early seventies. When Darwin died in 1882, he left an entire culture struggling to accommodate centuries of religious belief to his scientific discoveries. When Melville died in 1891, after 19 years of working in the Custom House in "this little shanty of an office", many believed he was already dead. He left his final masterpiece, *Billy-Budd,* in manuscript form to be published posthumously. It was well into this century before literary historians reinstated him. Only in the light of twentieth century literature perhaps, could we discern the lineaments of an American Kafka.

The fate of each man points a cautionary finger at the opposing fates of scientist and artist.

The Ape and the Whale is about two great nineteenth century geniuses, who dealt in their lives and works with problems so parallel that it is possible to construct a conversation between them using only their own words, as if they were both sitting in the same drawing room. They never met. But they traveled some of the same territory only a few years apart. Both were marvelous observers and brilliant descriptive writers. Each speculated on the origins of the human species and its possible apocalyptic fate. Each pondered the great questions about immortality and God.

The genesis of *The Ape and the Whale* was my realization* that Darwin and Melville were both in the Galápagos at roughly the same time: Darwin in 1835 and Melville in 1841. Both traveled to Polynesia. Looking further I discovered that they shared a passion for travel, for exploration, for natural history. Both were ambivalent about the theological beliefs of their age.

Their comments on similar subjects, sometimes agreeing, sometimes sharply disagreeing, gave me the feeling that I was overhearing a previously unheard conversation. The idea of an interplay, a dialogue, began to develop. Though they did not know each other, Melville at least knew something of Darwin. By 1847, after his own trip to the Galápagos, but before writing about them in "The Encantadas" in 1854, he had read *The Voyage of the Beagle*. As is evident in the lines from Clarel that open Act Two, Scene Three, Melville recognized that Darwin's thesis, if true, called into question the prevailing idea of a Providential Deity.

─────────────

*When researching *Nature and Culture* (Oxford University Press, 1980)

In this interplay, we accompany them (Act One) on their early travels from dour aridity to tropical verdure, from the Galápagos (Scene One) to Polynesia (Scene Two). At the outset, they both encounter with awe the famous tortoises, atavistic carriers of slow time. They then meet the native islanders around whom the first great dialogue about savage and civilization revolves.

In Act Two, Scene One, we are brought into the personal lives of two family men. Their remarks about and to their families are revelatory of their characters. For all his hesitancy—and somewhat Beckett-like monologue about marriage—Darwin seems to have been devoted to his children and to his wife Emma. She lovingly nurtured the semi-invalidism brought on by the mysterious chronic illness (possibly Chagas disease) for which he was scrubbed until red—"very like a lobster"—as he took cold water cures.

Melville's letter to his wife "Lizzie" (like Emma equally long-suffering in her concern for "Herman", his "morbid" sensitivity and his inability to find a job) is possibly the only one that survives. The rest are said to have been burned. His letter to his small son Malcolm reveals a tenderness rarely associated with him. It is made more poignant by his later letter to his brother-in-law, John C. Hoadley, referring to "Mackie's" death, a possible suicide at age eighteen, one of the profound tragedies of Melville's life. His complex emotional life is signalled also by his strange love for Nathaniel Hawthorne, an apparently unrequited passion that caused Hawthorne considerable embarrassment.

Act Two, Scene Two, sounds out Darwin and Melville's attitudes to their work and careers—especially to the two monumental books the effects of which continue to the present. Here Darwin's triumph and worldly success, despite initial obstacles, contrasts with Melville's disappointments and "failure".

As they move from the reception of the works to the works themselves—into the main theme of the ape and the whale—their extraordinary verbal anatomizations plunge us deep into the "stuff" of life and the implications of these biological ancestors for our own existence. Each man is obsessed with his respective animal, with the architecture of flesh and bone, with skins, tails, spines, brains, with horizontality and verticality, quadrupeds and bipeds, with the infinite pastures of sea or the regressive infinities of time.

Through these obsessions, articulated in scientific tones by Darwin, and more symbolically and poetically by Melville, they ultimately arrive (Act Two, Scene Three) at a level where they engage the notion of a Creator, speculate on God and madness, and ponder the enigma of immortality. The lifework of artist and scientist has led each to this mutual crescendo—to an existential questioning that, from their different perspectives, returns with puzzlement and grandeur to the origin of man and his ultimate fate. Now placed in the same space, each seems to overhear the other, to respond, to argue, to meditate, to share, to move together and apart as they revolve between them the themes that consumed them, and which we inherit, perhaps none the wiser.

Barbara Novak
New York City

Acknowledgments

We are extremely grateful to:

Yale University Press for permission to reprint material from Merrell R. Davis and William H. Gilman, eds. *The Letters of Herman Melville* (New Haven : 1960) Copyright 1960. Cambridge University Press for permission to reprint excerpts from Darwin's notes on marriage from Frederick Burckhardt and Sydney Smith eds., The *Correspondence of Charles Darwin*, vol. 2, 1837-1843. (Cambridge and New York: 1986). The Houghton Library, Harvard University, for permission to quote from Melville's poem," Pontoosuc" or "The Lake", [MS. AM188 (369.1.5)]. The Syndics of Cambridge University Library for permission to quote from Darwin's notebooks: Notebook B (Dar 121), Notebook M (Dar 125), Notebook N (Dar 126) and Darwin's abstract of John Macculloch (Dar 71) and to Georges Borchardt Inc. for permission to reprint the notebook material as transcribed by Paul H. Barrett, with commentary by Howard E. Gruber, in *Metaphysics, Materialism, & the Evolution of Mind, Early Writings of Charles Darwin* (Chicago: The University of Chicago Press,1974; Phoenix Edition 1980.)

Other sources fueling the dialogue of *The Ape and the Whale* included, for Herman Melville: *Moby-Dick* (1851),"The Encantadas", from *The Piazza Tales* (1856), *Typee* (1846) and *Clarel* (1876); for Charles Darwin: *The*

Voyage of the Beagle (6th edition, 1860), *The Descent of Man* (1871) and Francis Darwin ed. *The Life and Letters of Charles Darwin, Including an Autobiographical Chapter,* 2 vols. (1896).

The Ape and the Whale was first performed at Symphony Space on Upper Broadway, New York City on Sunday, March 28, 1987, as a benefit for Barnard College, through the kind encouragement of Ellen Futter, then President of Barnard, and the support of Richard and Gloria Manney, who were graceful and generous patrons. As directed by Isaiah Sheffer and performed by two brilliant actors, Stephen Lang (Melville) and David Margulies (Darwin), it set a magical model for all future performances. I am grateful to all of them for their dedication and commitment. I am also grateful to Maia Gregory, who encouraged its publication, to Carl Schreier, who made it a publication of the highest quality, and to my husband, Brian O'Doherty, without whose loving support my work and spirit would founder.

B.N.

THE APE & THE WHALE

ACT ONE

SCENE ONE
The Galápagos

MELVILLE

Take five-and-twenty heaps of cinders dumped here and there in an outside city lot; imagine some of them magnified into mountains, and the vacant lot the sea; and you will have a fit idea of the general aspect of the Encantadas, or Enchanted Isles. A group rather of extinct volcanoes than of isles; looking much as the world at large might, after a penal conflagration. It is to be doubted whether any spot of earth can, in desolateness, furnish a parallel to this group.

DARWIN

The *Beagle* sailed round Chatham Island, and anchored in several bays. One night I slept on shore on a part of the island, where black truncated cones were extraordinarily numerous: from one small eminence I counted sixty of them, all surmounted by craters more or less perfect.... The entire surface of this part of the island seems to have been permeated, like a sieve, by the subterranean vapours: here and there the lava, whilst soft, has been blown into great bubbles; and in other parts, the tops of caverns similarly formed have fallen in, leaving circular pits with steep sides.

MELVILLE

The special curse, as one may call it, of the Encantadas, is that to them change never comes; neither the change of seasons nor of sorrows. Cut by the Equator, they know not autumn and they know not spring; while already reduced to the lees of fire, ruin itself can work little more upon them. The showers refresh the deserts, but in these isles, rain never falls. Like split Syrian gourds, left withering in the sun, they are cracked by an everlasting drought beneath a torrid sky.... Another feature in these isles is their uninhabitableness. Man and wolf alike disown them. Little but reptile life is here found:—tortoises, lizards, immense spiders, snakes, and the strangest anomaly of outlandish Nature, the *aguano*. No voice, no low, no howl is heard; the chief sound of life here is a hiss.

DARWIN

Nothing could be less inviting than the first appearance. A broken field of black basaltic lava, thrown into the most rugged waves, and crossed by great fissures, is every where covered by stunted, sunburnt brushwood, which shows little signs of life. The dry and parched surface, being heated by the noonday sun, gave to the air a close and sultry feeling, like that from a stove: we fancied even that the bushes smelt unpleasantly. Although I diligently tried to collect as many plants as possible, I succeeded in getting very few; and such wretched-looking little weeds would have better become an arctic than an equatorial Flora.

MELVILLE

Concerning the peculiar reptile inhabitant of these wilds—whose presence gives the group its second Spanish name, Gallipagos—concerning the tortoises found here, most mariners have long cherished a superstition, not more frightful than grotesque. They earnestly believe that all wrecked sea-officers, more especially commodores and captains, are at death (and in some cases, before death) transformed into tortoises; thenceforth dwelling upon these hot aridities, sole solitary Lords of Asphaltum.

DARWIN

As I was walking along I met two large tortoises, each of which must have weighed at least two hundred pounds: one was eating a piece of cactus, and as I approached, it stared at me and slowly stalked away; the other gave a deep hiss, and drew in its head. These huge reptiles, surrounded by the black lava, the leafless shrubs, and large cacti, seemed to my fancy like some antediluvian animals.

MELVILLE

Some months before my first stepping ashore upon the group, my ship was cruising in its close vicinity. One noon we found ourselves off the South Head of Albemarle, and not very far from the land. Partly by way of freak, and partly by way of spying out so strange a country, a boat's crew was sent ashore, with orders to see all they could, and besides, bring back whatever tortoises they could conveniently transport. It was after sunset when the adventurers returned. I looked down over the ship's high side as if looking down over the curb of a well, and dimly saw the dump boat deep in the sea with some unwonted weight. Ropes were dropped over, and presently three huge antediluvian-looking tortoises, after much straining, were landed on deck. They seemed hardly of the seed of earth.

DARWIN

There can be little doubt that this tortoise is an aboriginal inhabitant of the Galápagos; for it is found on all, or nearly all, the islands, even on some of the smaller ones where there is no water; had it been an imported species, this would hardly have been the case in a group which has been so little frequented.

MELVILLE

We had been abroad upon the waters for five long months, a period amply sufficient to make all things of the land wear a fabulous hue to the dreamy mind. Had three Spanish custom-house officers boarded us then, it is not unlikely that I should have curiously stared at them, felt of them, and stroked them much as savages observe civilized guests. But instead of three custom-house officers, behold these really wondrous tortoises—none of your schoolboy mock turtles—but black as widower's weeds, heavy as chests of plate, with vast shells medallioned and orbed like shields, and dented and blistered like shields that have breasted a battle—shaggy too, here and there, with dark green moss, and slimy with the spray of the sea.

DARWIN

I will first describe the habits of the tortoise (Testudo nigra, formerly called Indica), which has been so frequently alluded to. These animals are found, I believe, on all the islands of the Archipelago; certainly on the greater number.

MELVILLE

These mystic creatures, suddenly translated by night from unutterable solitudes to our peopled deck, affected me in a manner not easy to unfold. They seemed newly crawled forth from beneath the foundations of the world. Yea, they seemed the identical tortoises whereon the Hindoo plants this total sphere. With a lantern I inspected them more closely. Such worshipful venerableness of aspect! Such furry greenness mantling the rude peelings and healing the fissures of their shattered shells. I no more saw three tortoises. They expanded—became transfigured. I seemed to see three Roman Coliseums in magnificent decay.

Ye oldest inhabitants of this or any other isle, said I, pray give me the freedom of your three-walled towns.

The great feeling inspired by these creatures was that of age:—dateless, indefinite endurance. And, in fact, that any other creature can live and breathe as long as the tortoise of the Encantadas, I will not readily believe. Not to hint of their known capacity of sustaining life, while going without food for an entire year, consider that impregnable armour of their living mail. What other bodily being possesses such a citadel wherein to resist the assaults of Time?

DARWIN

The tortoise is very fond of water, drinking large quantities, and wallowing in the mud. The larger islands alone possess springs, and those are always situated towards the central parts, and at a considerable height. The tortoises, therefore, which frequent the lower districts, when thirsty, are obliged to travel from a long distance. Hence broad and well-beaten paths branch off in every direction from the wells down to the sea-coast; and the Spaniards by following them up, first discovered the watering-places. When I landed at Chatham Island, I could not imagine what animal travelled so methodically along well chosen paths. Near the springs it was a curious spectacle to behold many of these huge creatures, one set eagerly travelling onwards with outstretched necks, and another set returning, after having drunk their fill. When the tortoise arrives at the spring, quite regardless of any spectator, he buries his head in the water above his eyes, and greedily swallows great mouthfuls, at the rate of about ten a minute.

MELVILLE

As I lay in my hammock that night, overhead I heard the slow, weary draggings of the three ponderous strangers along the encumbered deck. Their stupidity or their resolution was so great that they never went aside for any impediment. One ceased his movements altogether just before the midwatch. At sunrise I found him butted like a battering-ram against the immovable foot of the foremast, and still striving, tooth and nail, to force the impossible passage.

DARWIN

I believe it is well ascertained, that the bladder of the frog acts as a reservoir for the moisture necessary to its existence: such seems to be the case with the tortoise. For some time after a visit to the springs, their urinary bladders are distended with fluid, which is said gradually to decrease in volume, and to become less pure. The inhabitants, when walking in the lower district, and overcome with thirst, often take advantage of this circumstance, and drink the contents of the bladder if full: in one I saw killed, the fluid was quite limpid, and had only a slightly bitter taste. The inhabitants, however, always first drink the water in the pericardium, which is described as being best.

MELVILLE

That these tortoises are the victims of a penal, or malignant, or perhaps a downright diabolical enchanter, seems in nothing more likely than in that strange infatuation of hopeless toil which so often possesses them.

DARWIN

The tortoises, when purposely moving towards any point, travel by night and day, and arrive at their journey's end much sooner than would be expected. One large tortoise, which I watched, walked at the rate of sixty yards in ten minutes, that is 360 yards in the hour, or four miles a day,—allowing a little time for it to eat on the road. During the breeding season, when the male and female are together, the male utters a hoarse roar or bellowing, which, it is said, can be heard at the distance of more than a hundred yards. The female never uses her voice, and the male only at these times; so that when the people hear this noise, they know that the two are together....

The inhabitants believe that these animals are absolutely deaf; certainly they do not overhear a person walking close behind them. I was always amused when overtaking one of these great monsters, as it was quietly pacing along, to see how suddenly, the instant I passed, it would draw in its head and legs, and uttering a deep hiss fall to the ground with a heavy sound, as if struck dead. I frequently got on their backs, and then giving a few raps on the hinder part of their shells, they would rise up and walk away;—but I found it very difficult to keep my balance.

MELVILLE

In view of the description given, may one be gay upon the Encantadas? Yes: that is, find one the gaiety, and he will be gay. And indeed, sackcloth and ashes as they are, the isles are not perhaps unmitigated gloom. . . . even the tortoise, dark and melancholy as it is upon the back, still possesses a bright side; its calapee or breast-plate being sometimes of a faint yellowish or golden tinge. Moreover, every one knows that tortoises as well as turtles are of such a make, that if you but put them on their backs you thereby expose their bright sides without the possibility of their recovering themselves, and turning into view the other. But after you have done this, and because you have done this, you should not swear that the tortoise has no dark side. Enjoy the bright, keep it turned up perpetually if you can, but be honest and don't deny the black. . . . The tortoise is both black and bright.

SCENE TWO
Polynesia

MELVILLE

'Hurra, my lads! It's a settled thing; next week we shape our course to the Marquesas!' The Marquesas! What strange visions of outlandish things does not the very name spirit up! Naked houris—cannibal banquets —groves of cocoanut—coral reefs—tattooed chiefs— and bamboo temples; sunny valleys planted with bread-fruit-trees—carved canoes dancing on the flashing blue waters—savage woodlands guarded by horrible idols— *heathenish rites and human sacrifices.*

DARWIN

November 15th (1835).—At daylight, Tahiti, an island which must for ever remain classical to the voyager in the South Sea, was in view. At a distance the appearance was not attractive. The luxuriant vegetation of the lower part could not yet be seen, and as the clouds rolled past, the wildest and most precipitous peaks showed themselves towards the centre of the island.

MELVILLE

The vale was more than three leagues in length, and about a mile across at its greatest width.

On each side it appeared hemmed in by steep and green acclivities, which, uniting near the spot where I lay, formed an abrupt and semicircular termination of grassy cliffs and precipices hundreds of feet in height, over which flowed numberless small cascades.

DARWIN

As the evening drew to a close, I strolled beneath the gloomy shade of the bananas up the course of the stream. My walk was soon brought to a close, by coming to a waterfall between two and three hundred feet high; and again above this there was another. I mention all these waterfalls in this one brook, to give a general idea of the inclination of the land.

MELVILLE

Everywhere below me, from the base of the precipice upon whose very verge I had been unconsciously reposing, the surface of the vale presented a mass of foliage, spread with such rich profusion that it was impossible to determine of what description of trees it consisted.

But perhaps there was nothing about the scenery I beheld more impressive than those silent cascades, whose slender threads of water, after leaping down the steep cliffs, were lost amidst the rich herbage of the valley.

Over all the landscape there reigned the most hushed repose, which I almost feared to break, lest, like the enchanted gardens in the fairy tale, a single syllable might dissolve the spell.

DARWIN

In the little recess where the water fell, it did not appear that a breath of wind had ever blown.

MELVILLE

For a long time, forgetful alike of my own situation, and the vicinity of my still slumbering companion, I remained gazing around me, hardly able to comprehend by what means I had thus suddenly been made a spectator of such a scene.

DARWIN

From our position, almost suspended on the mountain-side, there were glimpses into the depths of the neighbouring valleys; and the lofty points of the central mountains, towering up within sixty degrees of the zenith, hid half the evening sky. Thus seated, it was a sublime spectacle to watch the shades of night gradually obscuring the last and highest pinnacles.

MELVILLE

A short time before my visit to the Marquesas, a somewhat amusing incident took place. . . which I cannot avoid relating.

An intrepid missionary, undaunted by the ill-success that had attended all previous endeavours to conciliate the savages, and believing much in the efficacy of female influence, introduced among them his young and beautiful wife, the first white woman who had ever visited their shores. The islanders at first gazed in mute admiration at so unusual a prodigy, and seemed inclined to regard it as some new divinity. But after a short time, becoming familiar with its charming aspect, and jealous of the folds which encircled its form, they sought to pierce the sacred veil of calico in which it was enshrined, and in the gratification of their curiosity so far overstepped the limits of good breeding, as deeply to offend the lady's sense of decorum. Her sex once ascertained, their idolatry was changed into contempt; and there was no end to the contumely showered upon her by the savages, who were exasperated at the deception which they conceived had been practised upon them. To the horror of her affectionate spouse, she was stripped of her garments, and given to understand that she could no longer carry on her deceits with impunity. The gentle dame was not sufficiently evangelical to endure this, and, fearful of further improprieties, she forced her husband to relinquish his undertaking, and together they returned to Tahiti.

DARWIN

As soon as we anchored in Matavai Bay, we were surrounded by canoes. This was our Sunday, but the Monday of Tahiti: if the case had been reversed, we should not have received a single visit; for the injunction not to launch a canoe on the sabbath is rigidly obeyed. After dinner we landed to enjoy all the delights produced by the first impressions of a new country, and that country the charming Tahiti. A crowd of men, women, and children, was collected on the memorable Point Venus, ready to receive us with laughing, merry faces. They marshalled us towards the house of Mr.

Wilson, the missionary of the district, who met us on the road, and gave us a very friendly reception. After sitting a short time in his house, we separated to walk about, but returned there in the evening.

MELVILLE

These celebrated warriors appear to inspire the other islanders with unspeakable terrors. Their very name is a frightful one; for the word "Typee" in the Marquesan dialect signifies a lover of human flesh. It is rather singular that the title should have been bestowed upon them exclusively, inasmuch as the natives of all this group are irreclaimable cannibals. The name may, perhaps, have been given to denote the peculiar ferocity of this clan, and to convey a special stigma along with it.

DARWIN

I was pleased with nothing so much as with the inhabitants. There is a mildness in the expression of their countenances which at once banishes the idea of a savage; and an intelligence which shows that they are advancing in civilization.

MELVILLE

I shall never forget the observation of one of our crew as we were passing slowly by the entrance of the bay. . . . As we stood gazing over the side at the verdant headlands, Ned, pointing with his hand in the direction of the treacherous valley, exclaimed, "There— there's Typee. Oh, the bloody cannibals, what a meal they'd make of us if we were to take it into our heads to land!

But they say they don't like sailor's flesh, it's too salt. I say, matey, how should you like to be shoved ashore there, eh?"

DARWIN

The common people, when working, keep the upper part of their bodies quite naked; and it is then that the Tahitians are seen to advantage. They are very tall, broad-shouldered, athletic, and well-proportioned. It has been remarked, that it requires little habit to make a dark skin more pleasing and natural to the eye of a European than his own colour.... Most of the men are tattooed, and the ornaments follow the curvature of the body so gracefully, that they have a very elegant effect. One common pattern, varying in its details, is somewhat like the crown of a palm-tree. It springs from the central line of the back, and gracefully curls round both sides. The simile may be a fanciful one, but I thought the body of a man thus ornamented was like the trunk of a noble tree embraced by a delicate creeper. . . .

MELVILLE

The old warrior...was arranging in round balls the two grey locks of hair that were suffered to grow from the crown of his head; his earrings and spear, both well polished, lay beside him, while the highly decorative pair of shoes hung suspended from a projecting cane against the side of the house. The young men were similarly employed; and the fair damsels, including Fayaway, were anointing themselves with "aka", arranging their long tresses, and performing other matters connected with the duties of the toilet.

DARWIN

Many of the elder people had their feet covered with small figures, so placed as to resemble a sock. This fashion, however, is partly gone by, and has been succeeded by others. Here, although fashion is far from immutable, every one must abide by that prevailing in his youth. An old man has thus his age for ever stamped on his body, and he cannot assume the airs of a young dandy.

MELVILLE

Having completed their preparations, the girls now exhibited themselves in gala costume; the most conspicuous feature of which was a necklace of beautiful white flowers, with the stems removed, and strung closely together upon a single fibre of tappa. Corresponding ornaments were inserted in their ears, and woven garlands upon their heads. About their waist they wore a short tunic of spotless white tappa, and some of them super-added to this a mantle of the same material, tied in an elaborate bow upon the left shoulder, and falling about the figure in picturesque folds.

Thus arrayed, I would have matched the charming Fayaway against any beauty in the world.

People may say what they will about the taste evinced by our fashionable ladies in dress. Their jewels, their feathers, their silks, and their furbelows, would have sunk into utter insignificance beside the exquisite simplicity of attire adopted by the nymphs of the vale on this festive occasion. I should like to have seen a gallery of coronation beauties, at Westminster Abbey, confronted for a moment by this band of Island girls;

their stiffness, formality, and affectation, contrasted with the artless vivacity and unconcealed natural graces of these savage maidens. It would be the Venus de' Medici placed beside a milliner's doll.

DARWIN

On the whole, it appears to me that the morality and religion of the inhabitants are highly creditable. There are many who attack...both the missionaries, their system, and the effects produced by it. Such reasoners never compare the present state with that of the island only twenty years ago; nor even with that of Europe at this day; but they compare it with the high standard of Gospel perfection.... They forget, or will not remember, that human sacrifices, and the power of an idolatrous priesthood—a system of profligacy unparalleled in any other part of the world—infanticide a consequence of that system—bloody wars, where the conquerors spared neither women nor children —that all these have been abolished; and that dishonesty, intemperance, and licentiousness have been greatly reduced by the introduction of Christianity. In a voyager to forget these things is base ingratitude; for should he chance to be at the point of shipwreck on some unknown coast, he will most devoutly pray that the lesson of the missionary may have extended thus far.

MELVILLE

The term "Savage" is, I conceive, often misapplied, and indeed, when I consider the vices, cruelties, and enormities of every kind that spring up in the tainted atmosphere of a feverish civilization, I am inclined to think that so far as the relative wickedness of the parties is concerned, four or five Marquesan Islanders sent to the United States as Missionaries might be quite as useful as an equal number of Americans dispatched to the Islands in a similar capacity.

I once heard it given as an instance of the frightful depravity of a certain tribe in the Pacific, that they had no word in their language to express the idea of virtue. The assertion was unfounded; but were it otherwise, it might be met by stating that their language is almost entirely destitute of terms to express the delightful ideas conveyed by our endless catalogue of civilized crimes.

DARWIN

From the varying accounts which I had read before reaching these islands, I was very anxious to form, from my own observation, a judgment of their moral state—although such judgment would necessarily be very imperfect. First impressions at all times very much depend on one's previously-acquired ideas.

MELVILLE

It will be urged that these shocking unprincipled wretches are cannibals. Very true; and a rather bad trait in their character it must be allowed. But they are such only when they seek to gratify the passion of revenge upon their enemies; and I ask whether the mere eating of human flesh so very far exceeds in barbarity that custom which only a few years since was practised in enlightened England:—a convicted traitor, perhaps a man found guilty of honesty, patriotism, and suchlike heinous crimes, had his head lopped off with a huge axe, his bowels dragged out and thrown into a fire; while his body, carved into four quarters, was with his head exposed upon pikes, and permitted to rot and fester among the public haunts of men!

The fiend-like skill we display in the invention of all manner of death-dealing engines, the vindictiveness with which we carry on our wars, and the misery and desolation that follow in their train, are enough of themselves to distinguish the white civilized man as the most ferocious animal on the face of the earth.

DARWIN

This day is reckoned in the log-book as Tuesday the 17th, instead of Monday the 16th, owing to our, so far, successful chase of the sun. Before breakfast the ship was hemmed in by a flotilla of canoes; and when the natives were allowed to come on board, I suppose there could not have been less than two hundred. It was the opinion of every one that it would have been difficult to have picked out an equal number from any other nation, who would have given so little trouble.

MELVILLE

One peculiarity that fixed my admiration was the perpetual hilarity reigning through the whole extent of the vale. There seemed to be no cares, griefs, troubles, or vexations, in all Typee. The hours tripped along as gaily as the laughing couples down a country dance.

DARWIN

Everybody brought something for sale: shells were the main article of trade.

MELVILLE

There were none of those thousand sources of irritation that the ingenuity of civilized man has created to mar his own felicity. There were no foreclosures of mortgages, no protested notes, no bills payable, no debts of honour in Typee; no unreasonable tailors and shoemakers, perversely bent on being paid; no duns of any description; no assault and battery attorneys, to foment discord, backing their clients up to a quarrel, and then knocking their heads together; no poor relations, everlastingly occupying the spare bed-chamber, and diminishing the elbow room at the family table; no destitute widows with their children starving on the cold charities of the world; no beggars; no debtors' prisons; no proud and hard-hearted nabobs in Typee; or to sum up all in one word—

DARWIN

The Tahitians now fully understand the value of money, and prefer it to old clothes or other articles.

MELVILLE

—no Money! "That root of all evil" was not to be found in the valley.

DARWIN

Of individual objects, perhaps nothing is more certain to create astonishment than the first sight in his native haunt of a barbarian,—of man in his lowest and most savage state. One's mind hurries back over past centuries, and then asks, could our progenitors have been men like these?—men, whose very signs and expressions are less intelligible to us than those of the domesticated animals; men, who do not possess the instinct of those animals, nor yet appear to boast of human reason, or at least of arts consequent on that reason.

MELVILLE

How often is the term "savages" incorrectly applied! None really deserving of it were ever yet discovered by voyagers or by travellers. They have discovered heathens and barbarians, whom by horrible cruelties they have exasperated into savages.

DARWIN

I do not believe it is possible to describe or paint the difference between savage and civilized man. It is the difference between a wild and tame animal: and part of the interest in beholding a savage, is the same which would lead every one to see the lion in his desert...

MELVILLE

It may be asserted without fear of contradiction, that in all the cases of outrages committed by Polynesians, Europeans have at some time or other been the aggressors, and that the cruel and bloodthirsty disposition of some of the islanders is mainly to be ascribed to the influence of such examples....

They whom we denominate "savages" are made to deserve the title. When the inhabitants of some sequestered island first descry the "big canoe" of the

European rolling through the blue waters towards their shores, they rush down to the beach in crowds, and with open arms stand ready to embrace the strangers. Fatal embrace! They fold to their bosom the vipers whose sting is destined to poison all their joys; and the instinctive feeling of love within their breast is soon converted to the bitterest hate....

Civilization does not engross all the virtues of humanity: she has not even her full share of them. They flourish in greater abundance and attain greater strength among many barbarous people....If truth and justice, and the better principles of our nature, cannot exist unless enforced by the statute-book, how are we to account for the social condition of the Typees? So pure and upright were they in all the relations of life, that entering their valley, as I did, under the most erroneous impressions of their character, I was soon led to exclaim in amazement: "Are these the ferocious savages, the blood-thirsty cannibals of whom I have heard such frightful tales! They deal more kindly with each other, and are more humane than many who study essays on virtue and benevolence, and who repeat every night that beautiful prayer breathed first by the lips of the divine and gentle Jesus." I will frankly declare that after passing a few weeks in this valley of the Marquesas, I formed a higher estimate of human nature than I had ever before entertained.

ACT TWO

SCENE ONE

Family & Friends

DARWIN

<u>Work finished</u>:

If <u>not</u> marry / Travel. Europe, yes? / America????

If I travel it must be exclusively geological United States, Mexico. Depend upon health & vigour & how far I become Zoological.

If I don't travel.— Work at transmission of Species—Microscope simplest forms of life—Geology? oldest formations?? Some experiments—physiological observation on lower animals. (B). Live in London for where else possible in small house, near Regents Park—keep horse—take Summer tours. Collect specimens some line of Zoolog[y]: Speculations of Geograph.[ical] range, & Geological general works.— Systematiz.— Study affinities.

<u>Work finished</u>:

If marry—means limited, Feel duty to work for money. London life, nothing but Society, no country,

no tours, no large Zoolog.[ical] Collect.[ion] no
books. Cambridge Professorship, either Geolog[y]
or Zoolog[y].— comply with all above requisites— I
could not systematiz[e] zoologically so well.— But better than hibernating in country, & where? Better even
than near London country house.— I could not indo-
lently take country house & do nothing— Could I live
in London like a prisoner? If I were moderately rich, I
would live in London, with pretty big house & do as (B),
but could I act thus with children & poor? No— Then
where live in country near London; better, but great
obstacles to science & poverty. Then Cambridge, better, but fish out of water, not being Professor & poverty. Then Cambridge Professorship,—& make best of
it, do duty as such & work at spare times—My destiny
will be Camb.[ridge] Prof.[essor] or poor man; outskirts
of London, some small Square & c.— & work as well as
I can.

I have so much more pleasure in direct observation, that I could not go on as Lyell does, correcting &
adding up new information to old train & I do not see
what line can be followed by man tied down to London.

In country, experiment & observations on lower
animals,—more space—

MELVILLE

Pittsfield

12 December 1850

My Dear Duyckinck:

If you expect a letter from a man who lives in the
country you must make up your mind to receive an

egotistical one—for he has no gossip nor news of any kind, unless his neighbor's cow has calved or the hen has laid a silver egg....

I have a sort of sea-feeling here in the country, now that the ground is all covered with snow. I look out my window in the morning when I rise as I would out of a port-hole of a ship in the Atlantic. My room seems a ship's cabin; & at nights when I wake up & hear the wind shrieking, I almost fancy there is too much sail on the house, & I had better go on the roof & rig in the chimney.

Do you want to know how I pass my time? —I rise at eight—thereabouts—& go to my barn—say good-morning to the horse, & give him his breakfast. (It goes to my heart to give him a cold one, but it can't be helped) Then, pay a visit to my cow—cut up a pumpkin or two for her, & stand by to see her eat it —for it's a pleasant sight to see a cow move her jaws—she does it so mildly & with such a sanctity.—My own breakfast over, I go to my workroom & light my fire—then spread my M.S.S. on the table—take one business squint at it, & fall to with a will. At 2½ P.M. I hear a preconcerted knock at my door, which (by request) continues till I rise & go to the door, which serves to wean me effectively from my writing, however interested I may be. My friends the horse & cow now demand their dinner—& I go and give it to them. My own dinner over, I rig my sleigh & with my mother or sisters start off for the village—& if it be a Literary World day, great is the satisfaction thereof.

DARWIN

—*Loss of time.*—cannot read in the evenings—

MELVILLE

My evenings I spend in a sort of mesmeric state in my room—not being able to read—only now & then skimming over some large-printed book....

Mrs. Melville with Malcolm is in Boston—or that lady would send her particular regards.

DARWIN

Not Marry.

Freedom to go where one liked— Choice of Society *& little of it.* Conversation of clever men at clubs.—

Not forced to visit relatives, & to bend in every trifle—to have the expense and anxiety of children—perhaps quarrelling.

MELVILLE

Jane & West Sts. /

Sep. 5, '77

Dear Cousin Kate:

You mention having spent a peaceful Sunday at Gansevoort, enjoying it much, with Abraham. I should have liked it well to have been of the company....—So it appears that I used in my letter to you the expression *"people of leisure."* If I did, it was a faulty expression.—as applied in that case. I doubtless meant people the disposition of whose time is not subject to another. But it amused me—your disclaiming the thing, as if there was any merit in *not* being a person of leisure.

Whoever is not in possession of leisure can hardly be said to possess independence. They talk of the *dignity of work*. Bosh. True Work is the *necessity* of poor humanity's earthly condition. The dignity is in leisure. Besides, 99 hundredths of all the *work* done in the world is either foolish and unnecessary, or harmful and wicked....

Bessie and the girls are doing well at the White Mountains, and will remain there yet for a time. Their absence makes it decidedly lonely often in the house.

Always affectionately

Yours

Cousin Herman

DARWIN

This is the Question:

Not Marry

No children, (no second life) no one to care for one in old age.—

What is the use of working without sympathy from near & dear friends—who are near and dear friends to the old, except *relatives*.

Marry

Children—(if it Please God)—Constant companion, (& friend in old age) who will feel interested in one, object to be beloved & played with—better than a dog anyhow—Home, & someone to take care of house—Charms of music & female chit-chat. These things good for one's health. Forced to visit & receive relations but *terrible loss of time*.

My God, it is intolerable to think of spending one's whole life, like a neuter bee, working, working & nothing after all,—No, no won't do.—

Imagine living all one's day solitarily in smoky dirty London House.—Only picture to yourself a nice soft wife on a sofa with good fire, & books & music perhaps—Compare this vision with the dingy reality of Grt Marlbro' St.

Marry—Marry—Marry Q.E.D.

MELVILLE

Sunday Afternoon / Washington

(To Elizabeth Shaw Melville), 24. 25 March 1861

My Dearest Lizzie:

I wrote you the other day from here, and now for another note. In the first place I must say that as yet I have been able to accomplish nothing in the matter of the consulship—have not in fact been able as yet so much as even to *see* any one on the subject. . . .

The night previous to this I was at the second levee at the White House. There was a great crowd, & a brilliant scene. Ladies in full dress by the hundred. A steady stream of two-&-two's wound thro' the apartments shaking hands with "Old Abe" and immediately passing on. This continued without cessation for an hour & a half. Of course I was one of the shakers. Old Abe is much better looking [than] I expected & younger looking. He shook hands like a good fellow—working hard at it like a man sawing wood at so much per cord. Mrs Lincoln is rather good-looking I thought. The scene was very fine altogether. Superb furniture—flood of light—magnificent flowers—full band of music &c. . . .

This morning I spent in the park opposite the White House, sunning myself on a seat. The grass is bright & beautiful, & the shrubbery beginning to bud. It is just cool enough to make an overcoat comfortable sitting out of doors. The wind is high however, & except in the parks, all is dust. I am boarding in a plain home—plain fare plain people. . . But if nothing else comes of it, I will at least derive good from the trip at this season. Though, to tell the truth, I feel homesick at times, strange as it may seem. How long I still remain is uncertain. I am expecting letters every day, & can do little or nothing till they arrive. . . .

Kisses to the children. Hope to get a letter from you today

Thine, My Dearest Lizzie

Herman

DARWIN

It being proved necessary to Marry—When? Soon or Late. The Governor says soon for otherwise bad if one has children—one's character is more flexible—one's feelings more lively, & if one does not marry soon, one misses so much good pure happiness.—

But then if I married tomorrow: there would be an infinity of trouble & expense in getting and furnishing a house,—fighting about no Society—morning calls—awkwardness— loss of time every day—(without one's wife was an angel & made one keep industrious).

MELVILLE

Sunday Evening, Dec. 2d 1860

My Dear Mrs. Morewood:

Lizzie has written you, I believe, that we purposed leaving for home on Monday (tomorrow) —but we have changed our plans. Lizzie and the children will remain here till Thursday; and I—in advance,—will go to Pittsfield on *Tuesday*, to get matters in readiness for them— putting up the stoves, airing the bedding— warming the house, and getting up a grand domestic banquet. I shall leave here in *the morning train on Tuesday*; and will be very happy to accept, for myself, your kind & neighborly invitation for a day or two. . . .

Very Truly & Sincerely

Your Friend & Neighbor

H Melville

—P.S. Very scratchy pen.

DARWIN

Few persons can have lived a more retired life than we have done. Besides short visits to the houses of relations, and occasionally to the seaside or elsewhere, we have gone nowhere.

MELVILLE

New York / 470 West St.

Day after Christmas, 1871

(To Peter Gansevoort)

Yesterday (Christmas) we all dined on Staten Island at Tom's, who gave us a bountiful and luxurious banquet.

DARWIN

During the first part of our residence we went a little into society, and received a few friends here; but my health almost always suffered from the excitement, violent shivering and vomiting attacks being thus brought on. I have therefore been compelled for many years to give up all dinner-parties; and this has been somewhat of a deprivation to me, as such parties always put me into high spirits.

MELVILLE

It was a big table, belted round by big appetites and bigger hearts, but the biggest of all...was at the head of the table—being big with satisfaction at seeing us enjoying ourselves. Mama looked uncommonly well; and Helen, Augusta, Kate (two Kates) Fanny, Minnie, Lottie, Frankie, Bessie, Fanny, Stanny, Mr. Hoadley, Mr. Griggs, not excluding the present modest writer—we all looked very well indeed.

DARWIN

From the same cause I have been able to invite here very few scientific acquaintances...I saw more of Lyell than of any other man, both before and after my marriage. His mind was characterised, as it appeared to me, by clearness, caution, sound judgment, and a good deal of originality. When I made any remark to him on Geology, he never rested until he saw the whole case clearly, and often made me see it more clearly than I had done before. He would advance all possible objections to my suggestion, and even after these were exhausted would long remain dubious. A second characteristic was his hearty sympathy with the work of other scientific men.

MELVILLE

Pittsfield

Nov. 17, 1851

(To Nathaniel Hawthorne)

Your letter was handed me last night on the road going to Mr. Morewood's, and I read it there. Had I been at home, I would have sat down at once and answered it. In me divine magnanimities are spontaneous and instantaneous—catch them while you can. The world goes round, and the other side comes up. So now I can't write what I felt. But I felt pantheistic then—your heart beat in my ribs and mine in yours, and both in God's. A sense of unspeakable security is in me this moment, on account of your having understood the book. I have written a wicked book and feel spotless as the lamb. Ineffable socialities are in me. I would sit down and dine with you and all the gods in old Rome's Pantheon. It is a strange feeling—no hopefulness is in it, no despair. Content—that is it; and irresponsibility; but without licentious inclination. I speak now of my profoundest sense of being, not of an incidental feeling.

Whence come you, Hawthorne? By what right do you drink from my flagon of life? And when I put it to my lips—lo, they are yours and not mine. I feel that the Godhead is broken up like the bread at the Supper, and that we are the pieces. Hence this infinite fraternity of feeling.

DARWIN

My first child was born on December 27, 1839, and I at once commenced to make notes on the first dawn of the various expressions which he exhibited, for I felt convinced, even at this early period, that the most complex and fine shades of expression must all have had a gradual and natural origin.

MELVILLE

Pacific Ocean (Off the coast of South America
On the Tropic of Capricorn)

Saturday   September 1st, 1860

(To Malcolm Melville (Mackie), age 11½.)

My Dear Malcolm: It is now three months exactly since the ship "Meteor" sailed from Boston—a quarter of a year. During this long period, she has been continually moving, and has only seen land on two days. I suppose you have followed out on the map (or my *globe* would be better—so you get Mama to clean it off for you) the route from Boston to San Francisco. The distance, by the straight track, is about 16000 miles; but the ship will have sailed before she gets there nearer to 18 or 20000 miles. So you see it is further than from the apple-tree to the big rock. When we crossed the Line in the Atlantic Ocean it was very warm; & we had warm weather for some weeks; but as we kept getting to the

Southward it began to grow less warm, and then cool-
ish, and cold and colder, till at last it was winter. I wore
two flannel shirts, and big mittens & overcoat, and a
great Russia cap, a very thick leather cap, so called by
sailors. . . .

DARWIN

Down, March 7th, 1852

(To W.D. Fox)

My dear Fox, —It is indeed an age since we have
had any communication, and very glad I was to receive
your note.... I congratulate and condole with you on
your *tenth* child; but please to observe when I have a
tenth, send only condolences to me. We now have seven
children, all well, thank God, as well as their mother; of
these seven, five are boys; and my father used to say
that it was certain that a boy gave as much trouble as three
girls; so that *bona fide* we have seventeen children.

MELVILLE

A very sad thing... happened the very morning we
were off the Cape—It was just about day-light; it was
blowing a gale of wind; and Uncle Tom ordered the top-
sails (big sails) to be furled. Whilst the sailors were aloft
on one of the yards, the ship rolled and plunged terri-
bly; and it blew with sleet and hail, and was very cold &
biting. Well, all at once, Uncle Tom saw something falling through the air, and then heard a thump, and then,—
looking before him, saw a poor sailor lying dead on the
deck. He had fallen from the yard, and was killed in-
stantly.—His shipmates picked him up, and carried him

under cover. By and by, when time could be spared, the sailmaker sewed up the body in a piece of sail-cloth, putting some iron balls—cannon balls—at the foot of it. And, when all was ready, the body was put on a plank, and carried to the ship's side in the presence of all hands. Then Uncle Tom, as Captain, read a prayer out of the prayer-book, and at a given word, the sailors who held the plank tipped it up, and immediately the body slipped into the stormy ocean, and we saw it no more.—Such is the way a poor sailor is buried at sea. This sailor's name was Ray. He had a friend among the crew; and they were both going to California, and thought of living there; but you see what happened. . . .

Pacific Ocean

On the Line, Sept. 16th, 1860

My Dear Malcolm:

The other day we saw a whale-ship; and I got into a boat and sailed over the ocean in it to the whale-ship, and stayed there about an hour. They had eight or ten of the "wild people" aboard. The Captain of the whale-ship had hired them at one of the islands called Roratonga. He wanted them to help pull in the whale-boat when they hunt the whale. . . .

DARWIN

What pleasant times we had in drinking coffee in your rooms at Christ's College, and think of the glories of the Crux-major. Ah, in those days there were no professions for sons, no ill-health to fear for them, no Californian gold, no French invasions. How paramount the future is to the present when one is surrounded by children. My dread is hereditary ill-health. Even death is better for them. My dear Fox, your sincere friend,

C. Darwin.

MELVILLE

—When we get to San Francisco, I shall put this letter in the post office there, and you will get it in about 25 days afterwards. It will go in a steamer to a place called Panama, on the Isthmus of Darien (get out your map, & find it) then it will cross the Isthmus by rail road to Aspinwall or Chagres on the Gulf of Mexico; there, another steamer will take it, which steamer, after touching at Havanna in Cuba for coals, will go direct to New York; and there, it will go to the Post Office, and so, get to Pittsfield. . . .

Now, my Dear Malcolm, I must finish my letter to you. I think of you, and Stanwix & Bessie and Fanny very often; and often long to be with you. But it can not be, at present. The picture which I have of you & the rest, I look at sometimes, till the faces almost seem real.—Now, my Dear Boy, good bye, & God bless you

Your affectionate father

H Melville

I enclose a little baby flying-fish's wing for Fanny. . .

By-by

Papa

[PAUSE]

DARWIN

Down, April 29th, 1851

My Dear Fox,— I do not suppose you will have heard of our bitter and cruel loss. Poor dear little Annie, when going on very well at Malvern, was taken with a vomiting attack, which was at first thought of the smallest importance; but it rapidly assumed the form of a low and dreadful fever, which carried her off in ten days. Thank God, she suffered hardly at all, and expired as tranquilly as a little angel. Our only consolation is that she passed a short, though joyous life. She was my favourite child; her cordiality, openness, buoyant joyousness and strong affections made her most loveable. Poor dear little soul. Well it is all over....

MELVILLE

To John Chipman Hoadley

Between 12 and 18 September 1867

New York

I wish you could have seen him as he lay in his last attitude, the ease of a gentle nature. Mackie never gave me a disrespectful word in his life, nor in any way ever failed in filialness.

SCENE TWO
The Work

MELVILLE

Pittsfield

June 1, 1851

(To Hawthorne)

In a week or so, I go to New York, to bury myself in a third-story room, and work and slave on my "Whale" while it is driving through the press. *That* is the only way I can finish it now,—I am so pulled hither and thither by circumstances. The calm, the coolness, the silent grass-growing mood in which a man *ought* always to compose,—that, I fear, can seldom be mine. Dollars damn me; and the malicious Devil is forever grinning in upon me, holding the door ajar. My dear Sir, a presentiment is on me,—I shall at last be worn out and perish, like an old nutmeg-grater, grated to pieces by the constant attrition of the wood, that is, the nutmeg.

DARWIN

In September 1858 I set to work by the strong advice of

Lyell and Hooker to prepare a volume on the transmutation of species, but was often interrupted by ill-health, and short visits to Dr. Lane's delightful hydropathic establishment at Moor Park. I abstracted the MS. begun on a much larger scale in 1856, and completed the volume on the same reduced scale. It cost me thirteen months and ten days' hard labour. It was published under the title of the *Origin of Species,* in November 1859. Though considerably added to and corrected in the later editions, it has remained substantially the same book.

It is no doubt the chief work of my life. It was from the first highly successful.

MELVILLE

What I feel most moved to write, that is banned, — it will not pay. Yet, altogether, write the *other* way I cannot. So the product is a final hash, and all my books are botches.

DARWIN

The first small edition of 1250 copies was sold on the day of publication, and a second edition of 3000 copies soon afterwards. Sixteen thousand copies have now (1876) been sold in England; and considering how stiff a book it is, this is a large sale. It has been translated into almost every European tongue, even into such languages as Spanish, Bohemian, Polish, and Russian. It has also. . . been translated into Japanese, and is there much studied. Even an essay in Hebrew has appeared on it, showing that the theory is contained in the Old Testament! The reviews were very numerous; for some time I collected all that appeared on the *Origin* and on my related books, and these amount (excluding news-paper reviews) to 265; but after a time I gave up the attempt in despair. Many separate essays and books on the subject have appeared; and in Germany a catalogue or bibliography on "Darwinismus" has appeared every year or two.

MELVILLE

But I was talking about the "Whale." As the fisher-men say, "he's in his flurry" when I left him some three weeks ago. I'm going to take him by his jaw, however, before long, and finish him up in some fashion or other. What's the use of elaborating what, in its very essence, is so short-lived as a modern book? Though I wrote the Gospels in this century, I should die in the gutter.

DARWIN

My books have sold largely in England, have been translated into many languages, and passed through several editions in foreign countries. I have heard it said that the success of a work abroad is the best test of its enduring value. I doubt whether this is at all trustwor-thy; but judged by this standard my name ought to last for a few years. Therefore it may be worth while to try to analyse the mental qualities and the conditions on which my success has depended; though I am aware that no man can do this correctly.

I have no great quickness of apprehension or wit which is so remarkable in some clever men, for instance, Huxley. I am therefore a poor critic: a paper or book, when first read, generally excites my admiration, and it is only after considerable reflection that I perceive the weak points. My power to follow a long and purely abstract train of thought is very limited; and therefore I could never have succeeded with metaphysics or mathematics. My memory is extensive, yet hazy: it suffices to make me cautious by vaguely telling me that I have observed or read something opposed to the conclusion which I am drawing, or on the other hand in favour of it; and after a time I can generally recollect where to search for my authority. So poor in one sense is my memory, that I have never been able to remember for more than a few days a single date or a line of poetry.

Some of my critics have said, "Oh, he is a good observer, but he has no power of reasoning!" I do not think that this can be true, for the *Origin of Species* is one long argument from the beginning to the end, and it has convinced not a few able men. No one could have written it without having some power of reasoning. I have a fair share of invention, and of common sense and judgment, such as every fairly successful lawyer or doctor must have, but not, I believe, in any higher degree.

On the favourable side of the balance, I think that I am superior to the common run of men in noticing things which easily escape attention, and in observing them carefully. My industry has been nearly as great as it could have been in the observation and collection of facts. What is far more important, my love of natural science has been steady and ardent.

MELVILLE

My development has been all within a few years past. I am like one of those seeds taken out of the Egyptian Pyramids which, after being three thousand years a seed and nothing but a seed, being planted in English soil, it developed itself, grew to greenness, and then fell to mould. So I. Until I was twenty-five, I had no development at all. From my twenty-fifth year I date my life. Three weeks have scarcely passed, at any time between then and now, that I have not unfolded within myself. But I feel that I am now come to the inmost leaf of the bulb, and that shortly the flower must fall to the mould.

DARWIN

My habits are methodical, and this has been of...use for my particular line of work. Lastly, I have had ample leisure from not having to earn my own bread. Even ill-health, though it has annihilated several years of my life, has saved me from the distractions of society and amusement.

Therefore, my success as a man of science, whatever this may have amounted to, has been determined, as far as I can judge, by complex and diversified mental qualities and conditions. Of these, the most important have been—the love of science—unbounded patience in long reflecting over any subject—industry in observing and collecting facts—and a fair share of invention as well as of common-sense. With such moderate abilities as I possess, it is truly surprising that I should have influenced to a considerable extent the belief of scientific men on some important points.

MELVILLE

(To Nathaniel Hawthorne)

I was in New York for four-and-twenty hours the other day, and saw a portrait of N.H. And I have seen and heard many flattering (in a publisher's point of view) allusions to the "Seven Gables." And I have seen "Tales" and "A New Volume" announced, by N.H. So upon the whole, I say to myself, this N.H. is in the ascendant. My dear Sir, they begin to patronize. All Fame is patronage. Let me be infamous; there is no patronage in *that*. What "reputation" H.M. has is horrible. Think of it! To go down to posterity is bad enough, any way; but to go down as a "man who lived among the cannibals"!

DARWIN

I have almost always been treated honestly by my reviewers, passing over those without scientific knowledge as not worthy of notice. My views have often been grossly misinterpreted, bitterly opposed and ridiculed, but this has been generally done as I believe, in good faith. On the whole I do not doubt that my works have been over and over again greatly overpraised....

The success of the *Origin* may, I think, be attributed in large part to my having long before written two condensed sketches, and to my having finally abstracted a much larger manuscript, which was itself an abstract. By this means I was enabled to select the more striking facts and conclusions. I had, also, during many years, followed a golden rule, namely, that whenever a published fact, a new observation or thought came across me, which was opposed to my general results, to make a memorandum of it without fail and at once; for I had found by experience that such facts and thoughts were far more apt to escape from the memory than favourable ones. Owing to this habit, very few objections were raised against my views which I had not at least noticed and attempted to answer....

Another element in the success of the book was its moderate size; and this I owe to the appearance of Mr. Wallace's essay; had I published on the scale in which I began to write in 1856, the book would have been four or five times as large as the *Origin,* and very few would have had the patience to read it.

I gained much by my delay in publishing from about 1839, when the theory was clearly conceived, to 1859; and I lost nothing by it, for I cared very little whether men attributed most originality to me or Wallace; and his essay no doubt aided in the reception of the theory.

MELVILLE

One often hears of writers that rise and swell with their subject, though it may seem but an ordinary one. How, then, with me, writing of this Leviathan? Unconsciously my chirography expands into placard capitals. Give me a condor's quill! Give me Vesuvius' crater for an inkstand! Friends, hold my arms! For in the mere act of penning my thoughts of this Leviathan, they weary me, and make me faint with their outreaching comprehensiveness of sweep, as if to include the whole circle of the sciences, and all the generations of whales, and men, and mastodons, past, present, and to come, with all the revolving panoramas of empire on earth, and throughout the universe, not excluding its suburbs. Such, and so magnifying, is the virtue of a large and liberal theme! We expand to its bulk. To produce a mighty book, you must choose a mighty theme. No great and enduring volume can ever be written on the flea, though many there be who have tried it.

DARWIN

To describe the habits and mental powers of worker-ants, would require, as Pierre Huber has shewn, a large volume. . . Ants certainly communicate information to each other, and several unite for the same work, or for games of play. They recognise their fellow-ants after months of absence, and feel sympathy for each other. They build great edifices, keep them clean, close the doors in the evening, and post sentries. They make roads as well as tunnels under rivers, and temporary bridges over them, by clinging together. They collect food for the community, and when an object, too large for entrance, is brought to the nest, they enlarge the door, and afterwards build it up again. They store up seeds, of which they prevent the germination, and which, if damp, are brought up to the surface to dry. They keep aphides and other insects as milch-cows. They go out to battle in regular bands, and freely sacrifice their lives for the common weal. They emigrate according to preconcerted plan. They capture slaves. They move the eggs of their aphides, as well as their own eggs and cocoons, into warm parts of the nest, in order that they may be quickly hatched; and endless similar facts could be given.

+ p. 76

MELVILLE

Now the various species of whales need some sort of popular comprehensive classification, if only an easy outline one for the present, hereafter to be filled in all its departments by subsequent laborers.

As no better man advances to take this matter in hand, I hereupon offer my own poor endeavors. I promise nothing complete; because any human thing supposed to be complete, must for that very reason infallibly be faulty.

DARWIN

The grand Question which every naturalist ought to have before him when dissecting a whale or classifying a mite, a fungus or an infusorian is "What are the Laws of Life[?]"

MELVILLE

First: According to magnitude I divide the whales into three primary BOOKS (subdivisible into Chapters), and these shall comprehend them all, both small and large.

I. The Folio Whale; II. the Octavo Whale; III. the Duodecimo Whale.

As the type of the Folio I present the *Sperm Whale;* of the Octavo, the *Grampus;* of the Duodecimo, the *Porpoise.*

FOLIOS. Among these I here include the following chapters:—I. the *Sperm Whale;* II. the *Right Whale;* III. the *Fin-Back Whale;* IV. the *Humpbacked Whale;* V. the *Razor-Back Whale;* VI. the *Sulphur Bottom Whale.*

BOOK I. (*Folio*), Chapter I. (*Sperm Whale*). —This whale, among the English of old vaguely known as the Trumpa Whale, and the Physeter Whale, and the Anvil Headed Whale, is the present Cachalot of the French, and the Pottfisch of the Germans, and the Macrocephalus of the Long Words. He is, without doubt, the largest inhabitant of the globe; the most formidable of all whales to encounter; the most majestic in aspect;

and lastly, by far the most valuable in commerce; he being the only creature from which that valuable substance, spermaceti, is obtained.

DARWIN

I may mention that I keep from thirty to forty large portfolios, in cabinets with labelled shelves, into which I can at once put a detached reference or memorandum. I have bought many books, and at their ends I make an index of all the facts that concern my work; or, if the book is not my own, write out a separate abstract, and of such abstracts I have a large drawer full. Before beginning on any subject I look to all the short indexes and make a general and classified index, and by taking the one or more proper portfolios I have all the information collected during my life ready for use.

MELVILLE

It is a ponderous task; no ordinary lettersorter in the Post-office is equal to it. To grope down into the bottom of the sea after them; to have one's hands among the unspeakable foundations, ribs, and very pelvis of the world; this is a fearful thing. What am I that I should essay to hook the nose of this Leviathan! The awful tauntings in Job might well appall me. "Will he (the Leviathan) make a covenant with thee? Behold the hope of him is vain!" But I have swam through libraries and sailed through oceans; I have had to do with whales with these visible hands; I am in earnest; and I will try. There are some preliminaries to settle.

First: the uncertain, unsettled condition of this science of Cetology is in the very vestibule attested by the fact, that in some quarters it still remains a moot point whether a whale be a fish. In his System of Nature, A.D. 1776, Linnæus declares, "I hereby separate the whales from the fish." But of my own knowledge, I know that down to the year 1850, sharks and shad, alewives and herring, against Linnæus's express edict, were still found dividing the possession of the same seas with the Leviathan.

The grounds upon which Linnæus would fain have banished the whales from the waters, he states as follows: "On account of their warm binocular heart, their lungs, their movable eyelids, their hollow ears, penem intrantem feminam mammis lactanem," and finally, "ex lege naturæ jure meritoque." I submitted all this to my friends Simeon Macey and Charley Coffin, of Nantucket, both messmates of mine in a certain voyage, and they united in the opinion that the reasons set forth were altogether insufficient. Charley profanely hinted they were humbug.

Be it known that, waiving all argument, I take the good old fashioned ground that the whale is a fish, and call upon holy Jonah to back me. This fundamental thing settled, the next point is, in what internal respect does the whale differ from other fish. Above, Linnæus has given you those items. But in brief, they are these: lungs and warm blood; whereas, all other fish are lungless and cold blooded.

Next: how shall we define the whale, by his obvious externals, so as conspicuously to label him for all time to come? To be short, then, a whale is *a spouting fish with a horizontal tail*. There you have him. However contracted, that definition is the result of expanded meditation.

DARWIN

Do the Ourang Outang like smells / peppermint / & music / Have the monkeys lice?—

Do female monkeys not show signs of impatience when women present?

Do they pout, or spit, or cry.—. . .

Do female monkeys care for men.—

[PAUSE]

MELVILLE

The question is, what and where is the skin of the whale? Already you know what his blubber is. That blubber is something of the consistence of firm, close-grained beef, but tougher, more elastic and compact, and ranges from eight or ten to twelve and fifteen inches in thickness.

DARWIN

Another most conspicuous difference between man and the lower animals is the nakedness of his skin. Whales and porpoises (Cetacea), dugongs (Sirenia) and the hippopotamus are naked; and this may be advantageous for them for gliding through the water; nor would it be injurious to them from the loss of warmth, as the species which inhabit the colder regions, are protected by a thick layer of blubber, serving the same purpose as the fur of seals and otters.

MELVILLE

Now, however, preposterous it may first seem to talk of any creature's skin as being of that sort of consistence and thickness, yet in point of fact these are no arguments against such a presumption; because you cannot raise any other dense enveloping layer from the whale's body but that same blubber; and the outermost enveloping layer of any animal, if reasonably dense, what can that be but the skin? True, from the unmarred dead body of the whale, you may scrape off with your hand an infinitely thin, transparent substance, somewhat resembling the thinnest shreds of isinglass, only it is almost as flexible and soft as satin; that is, previous to being dried, when it not only contracts and thickens, but becomes rather hard and brittle. I have several such dried bits, which I use for marks in my whale-books. It is transparent, as I said before; and being laid upon the printed page, I have sometimes pleased myself with fancying it exerted a magnifying influence. At any rate, it is pleasant to read about whales through their own spectacles, as you may say. But what I am driving at here is this. That same infinitely thin, isinglass substance, which, I admit, invests the entire body of the whale, is not so much to be regarded as the skin of the creature, as the skin of the skin, so to speak; for it were simply ridiculous to say, that the proper skin of the tremendous whale is thinner and more tender than the skin of a new-born child.

DARWIN

Man differs conspicuously from all the other Primates in being almost naked.

MELVILLE

In life, the visible surface of the Sperm Whale is not the least among the many marvels he presents. Almost invariably it is all over obliquely crossed and recrossed with numberless straight marks in thick array, something like those in the finest Italian line engravings. But these marks do not seem to be impressed upon the isinglass substance above mentioned, but seem to be seen through it, as if they were engraved upon the body itself. Nor is this all. In some instances, to the quick, observant eye, those linear marks, as in a veritable engraving, but afford the ground for far other delineations. These are hieroglyphical; that is, if you call those mysterious cyphers on the walls of pyramids hieroglyphics, then that is the proper word to use in the present connexion. By my retentive memory of the hieroglyphics upon one Sperm Whale in particular, I was much struck with a plate representing the old Indian characters chiselled on the famous hieroglyphic palisades on the banks of the Upper Mississippi. Like those mystic rocks, too, the mystic-marked whale remains undecipherable.

DARWIN

...a few straggling hairs are found over the greater part of the body in the man, and fine down on that of a woman. The different races differ much in hairiness; and in the individuals of the same race the hairs are highly variable, not only in abundance, but likewise in position: thus in some Europeans the shoulders are quite naked, whilst in others they bear thick tufts of hair. There can be little doubt that the hairs thus scattered over the body are the rudiments of the uniform hairy coat of the lower animals. . . the woolly covering of the fœtus probably represents the first permanent coat of hair in those mammals which are born hairy.

[PAUSE]

MELVILLE

Other poets have warbled the praises of the soft eye of the antelope, and the lovely plumage of the bird that never alights; less celestial, I celebrate a tail.

Reckoning the largest sized Sperm Whale's tail to begin at that point of the trunk where it tapers to about the girth of a man, it comprises upon its upper surface alone, an area of at least fifty square feet. The compact round body of its root expands into two broad, firm, flat palms or flukes, gradually shoaling away to less than an inch in thickness. At the crotch or junction, these flukes slightly overlap, then sideways recede from each other like wings, leaving a wide vacancy between. In no living things are the lines of beauty more exquisitely defined than in the crescentic borders of these flukes. At its utmost expansion in the full grown whale, the tail will considerably exceed twenty feet across.

DARWIN

In man, the os coccyx, together with certain other vertebræ hereafter to be described, though function-less as a tail, plainly represent this part in other verte-brate animals. At an early embryonic period it is free, and projects beyond the lower extremities; as may be seen in the drawing of a human embryo. Even after birth it has been known, in certain rare and anomalous cases, to form a small external rudiment of a tail.

MELVILLE

The entire member seems a dense webbed bed of welded sinews; but cut into it, and you find that three distinct strata compose it:—upper, middle, and lower. The fibres in the upper and lower layers, are long and horizontal; those of the middle one, very short, and running crosswise between the outside layers. This triune structure, as much as anything else, imparts power to the tail. To the student of old Roman walls, the middle layer will furnish a curious parallel to the thin course of tiles always alternating with the stone in those wonderful relics of the antique, and which undoubtedly contribute so much to the great strength of the masonry.

But as if this vast local power in the tendinous tail were not enough, the whole bulk of the Leviathan is knit over with a warp and woof of muscular fibres and filaments, which passing on either side the loins and running down into the flukes, insensibly blend with them, and largely contribute to their might; so that in the tail the confluent measureless force of the whole whale seems concentrated to a point. Could annihilation occur to matter, this were the thing to do it.

DARWIN

The os coccyx is short, usually including only four vertebræ, all anchylosed together: and these are in a rudimentary condition, for they consist, with the exception of the basal one, of the centrum alone. They are furnished with some small muscles; one of which, as I am informed by Prof. Turner, has been expressly described by Theile as a rudimentary repetition of the extensor of the tail, a muscle which is so largely developed in many mammals.

MELVILLE

Such is the subtle elasticity of the organ I treat of, that whether wielded in sport, or in earnest, or in anger, whatever be the mood it be in, its flexions are invariably marked by exceeding grace. Therein no fairy's arm can transcend it....

Being horizontal in its position, the Leviathan's tail acts in a different manner from the tails of all other sea creatures. It never wriggles. In man or fish, wriggling is a sign of inferiority. To the whale, his tail is the sole means of propulsion. Scroll-wise coiled forwards beneath the body, and then rapidly sprung backwards, it is this which gives that singular darting, leaping motion to the monster when furiously swimming. His side-fins only serve to steer by....

I cannot demonstrate it, but it seems to me, that in the whale the sense of touch is concentrated in the tail; for in this respect there is a delicacy in it equalled only by the daintiness of the elephant's trunk. This delicacy is chiefly evinced in the action of sweeping, when in maidenly gentleness the whale with a certain soft slowness moves his immense flukes from side to side upon the surface of the sea; and if he feel but a sailor's whisker, woe to that sailor, whiskers and all. What tenderness there is in that preliminary touch!

DARWIN

According to a popular impression, the absence of a tail is eminently distinctive of man; but as those apes which come nearest to him are destitute of this organ, its disappearance does not relate exclusively to man.... A tail, though not externally visible, is really present in man and the anthropomorphous apes, and is constructed on exactly the same pattern in both.

MELVILLE

The more I consider this mighty tail, the more do I deplore my inability to express it. At times there are gestures in it, which, though they would well grace the hand of man, remain wholly inexplicable. In an extensive herd, so remarkable, occasionally, are these mystic gestures, that I have heard hunters who have declared them akin to Free-Mason signs and symbols; that the whale, indeed, by these methods intelligently conversed with the world. Nor are there wanting other motions of the whale in his general body, full of strangeness, and unaccountable to his most experienced assailant. Dissect him how I may, then, I but go skin deep; I know him not, and never will. But if I know not even the tail of this whale, how understand his head? much more, how comprehend his face, when face he has none? Thou shalt see my back parts, my tail, he seems to say, but my face shall not be seen. But I cannot completely make out his back parts; and hint what he will about his face, I say again he has no face.

DARWIN

But what are we to say about the rudimentary and variable vertebræ of the terminal portion of the tail, forming the os coccyx? A notion which has often been, and will no doubt again be ridiculed, namely, that friction has had something to do with the disappearance of the external portion of the tail, is not so ridiculous as it at first appears....

As we now have evidence that mutilations occasionally produce an inherited effect, it is not very improbable that in short-tailed monkeys, the projecting part of the tail, being functionally useless, should after many generations have become rudimentary and distorted, from being continually rubbed and chaffed.... Finally, then, as far as we can judge, the tail has disappeared in man and the anthropomorphous apes, owing to the terminal portion having been injured by friction during a long lapse of time; the basal and embedded portion having been reduced and modified, so as to become suitable to the erect or semi-erect position.

[PAUSE]

MELVILLE

In the case of a small Sperm Whale the brains are accounted a fine dish. The casket of the skull is broken into with an axe, and the two plump, whitish lobes being withdrawn (precisely resembling two large puddings), they are then mixed with flour, and cooked into a most delectable mess, in flavor somewhat resembling calves' head which is quite a dish among some epicures; and every one knows that some young bucks among the epicures, by continually dining upon calves' brains, by and by get to have a little brains of their own, so as to be able to tell a calf's head from their own heads; which, indeed, requires uncommon discrimination. And that is the reason why a young buck with an intelligent looking calf's head before him, is somehow one of the saddest sights you can see. The head looks a sort of reproachfully at him, with an "Et tu Brute!" expression.

DARWIN

That my mind became developed through my pursuits during the voyage [of the Beagle] is rendered probable by a remark made by my father, who was the most acute observer whom I ever saw, of a sceptical disposition, and far from being a believer in phrenology; for on first seeing me after the voyage, he turned round to my sisters, and exclaimed, "Why, the shape of his head is quite altered."

MELVILLE

Phrenologically the head of this Leviathan, in the creature's living intact state, is an entire delusion. As for his true brain, you can then see no indications of it, nor feel any. The whale, like all things that are mighty, wears a false brow to the common world.

If you unload his skull of its spermy heaps and then take a rear view of its rear end, which is the high end, you will be struck by its resemblance to the human skull, beheld in the same situation, and from the same point of view. Indeed, place this reversed skull (scaled down to the human magnitude) among a plate of men's skulls, and you would involuntarily confound it with them; and remarking the depressions on one part of its summit, in phrenological phrase you would say—This man had no self-esteem, and no veneration.

DARWIN

No one supposes that the intellect of any two animals or of any two men can be accurately gauged by the cubic contents of their skulls. It is certain that there may be extraordinary mental activity with an extremely small absolute mass of nervous matter: thus the wonderfully diversified instincts, mental powers, and affectations of ants are notorious, yet their cerebral ganglia are not so large as the quarter of a small pin's head. Under this point of view, the brain of an ant is one of the most marvellous atoms of matter in the world, perhaps more so than the brain of man.

MELVILLE

If the Sperm Whale be physiognomically a Sphinx to the phrenologist his brain seems that geometrical circle which it is impossible to square.

In the full-grown creature the skull will measure at least twenty feet in length. Unhinge the lower jaw, and the side view of his skull is as the side view of a moderately inclined plane resting throughout on a level base. But in life—as we have elsewhere seen—this inclined plane is angularly filled up, and almost squared by the enormous super-incumbent mass of the junk and sperm. At the high end the skull forms a crater to bed that part of the mass; while under the long floor of this crater—in another cavity seldom exceeding ten inches in length and as many in depth—reposes the mere handful of this monster's brain. The brain is at least twenty feet from his apparent forehead in life; it is hidden away behind its vast outworks, like the innermost citadel within the amplified fortifications of Quebec. So like a choice casket is it secreted in him, that I have known some whalemen who peremptorily deny that the Sperm Whale has any other brain than that palpable semblance of one formed by the cubic-yards of his sperm magazine.

DARWIN

The gradually increasing weight of the brain and skull in man must have influenced the development of the supporting spinal column, more especially whilst he was becoming erect.

[PAUSE]

MELVILLE

Go to the meatmarket of a Saturday night and see the crowds of live bipeds staring up at the long rows of dead quadrupeds. Does not that sight take a tooth out of the cannibal's jaw? Cannibals? who is not a cannibal? I tell you it will be more tolerable for the Fejee that salted down a lean missionary in his cellar against a coming famine; it will be more tolerable for that provident Fejee, I say, in the day of judgment, than for thee, civilized and enlightened gourmand, who nailest geese to the ground and feasted on their bloated livers in thy paté-de-foie-gras.

DARWIN

As soon as some ancient member in the great series of the Primates came to be less arboreal, owing to a change in its manner of procuring subsistence, or to some change in the surrounding conditions, its habitual manner of progression would have been modified: and thus it would have been rendered more strictly quadrupedal or bipedal. Baboons frequent hilly and rocky districts, and only from necessity climb high trees; and they have acquired almost the gait of a dog. Man alone has become a biped; and we can, I think, partly see how he has come to assume his erect attitude, which forms one of his most conspicuous characters. Man could not have attained his present dominant position in the world without the use of his hands, which are so admirably adapted to act in obedience to his will. . . . But the hands and arms could hardly have become perfect enough to have manufactured weapons, or to have hurled stones and spears with a true aim, as long as they were habitually used for locomotion and for supporting the whole weight of the body, or, as before remarked, so long as they were especially fitted for climbing trees. Such rough treatment would also have blunted the sense of touch, on which their delicate use largely depends. From these causes alone it would have been an advantage to man to become a biped; but for many actions it is indispensable that the arms and whole upper part of the body should be free; and he must for this end stand firmly on his feet.

MELVILLE

If you attentively regard almost any quadruped's spine, you will be struck with the resemblance of its vertebræ to a strung necklace of dwarfed skulls, all bearing rudimental resemblance to the skull proper. It is a German conceit, that the vertebræ are absolutely undeveloped skulls. . . . Now, I consider that the phrenologists have omitted an important thing in not pushing their investigations from the cerebellum through the spinal canal. For I believe that much of a man's character will be found betokened in his backbone. I would rather feel your spine than your skull, whoever you are. A thin joist of a spine never yet upheld a full and noble soul. I rejoice in my spine, as in the firm audacious staff of that flag which I fling half out to the world.

DARWIN

The most ancient progenitors in the kingdom of the Vertebrata, at which we are able to obtain an obscure glance, apparently consisted of a group of marine animals, resembling the larvæ of existing Ascidians. These animals probably gave rise to a group of fishes, as lowly organised as the lancelet; and from these the Ganoids, and other fishes like Lepidosiren, must have been developed. From such fish a very small advance would carry us on to the Amphibians. We have seen that birds and reptiles were once intimately connected together; and the Monotremata now connect mammals with reptiles in a slight degree. But no one can at present say by what line of descent the three higher and related classes, namely, mammals, birds, and reptiles, were derived from the two lower vertebrate classes, namely, amphibians and fishes. In the class of mammals the steps are not difficult to conceive which led from the ancient Monotremata to the ancient Marsupials; and from these to the early progenitors of the placental mammals. We may thus ascend to the Lemuridæ; and the interval is not very wide from these to the Simiadæ. The Simiadæ then branched off into two great stems, the New World and Old World monkeys; and from the latter, at a remote period, Man, the wonder and glory of the Universe, proceeded.

MELVILLE

In length, the Sperm Whale's skeleton at Tranque measured seventy-two feet; so that when fully invested and extended in life, he must have been ninety feet long; for in the whale, the skeleton loses about one fifth in length compared with the living body. Of this seventy-two feet, his skull and jaw comprised some twenty feet, leaving some fifty feet of plain backbone. Attached to this back-bone, for something less than a third of its length, was the mighty circular basket of ribs which once enclosed his vitals.

DARWIN

Thus we have given to man a pedigree of prodigious length, but not, it may be said, of noble quality. The world, it has often been remarked, appears as if it had long been preparing for the advent of man: and this, in one sense is strictly true, for he owes his birth to a long line of progenitors. If any single link in this chain had never existed, man would not have been exactly what he now is. Unless we wilfully close our eyes, we may, with our present knowledge, approximately recognise our parentage; nor need we feel ashamed of it. The most humble organism is something much higher than the inorganic dust under our feet; and no one with an unbiased mind can study any living creature, however humble, without being struck with enthusiasm at its marvellous structure and properties.

MELVILLE

But the spine. For that, the best way we can consider it is, with a crane, to pile its bones up on end. No speedy enterprise. But now it's done, it looks much like Pompey's Pillar.

There are forty and odd vertebræ in all, which in the skeleton are not locked together. They mostly lie like the great knobbed blocks on a Gothic spire, forming solid courses of heavy masonry. The largest, a middle one, is in width something less than three feet, and in depth more than four. The smallest, where the spine tapers away into the tail, is only two inches in width, and looks something like a white billiard-ball. I was told there were still smaller ones, but they had been lost by some little cannibal urchins, the priest's children, who had stolen them to play marbles with. Thus we see how that the spine of even the hugest of living things tapers off at last into simple child's play.

SCENE THREE
God, Madness & Immortality

MELVILLE

If Luther's day expand to Darwin's year,
Shall that exclude the hope—foreclose the
    fear? . . .

Yea, ape and angel, strife and old debate—
The harps of heaven and dreary gongs of hell;
Science and feud can only aggravate—
No umpire she betwixt the chimes and knell:
The running battle of the star and clod
Shall run for ever—if there be no God.

DARWIN

The belief in God has often been advanced as not
only the greatest, but the most complete of all the dis-
tinctions between man and the lower animals. It is however impossible, as we have seen, to maintain that this

belief is innate or instinctive in man. On the other hand
a belief in all-pervading spiritual agencies seems to be
universal; and apparently follows from a considerable
advance in man's reason, and from a still greater advance in his faculties of imagination, curiosity and wonder. I am aware that the assumed instinctive belief in
God has been used by many persons as an argument
for His existence. But this is a rash argument, as we
should thus be compelled to believe in the existence of
many cruel and malignant spirits, only a little more
powerful than man; for the belief in them is far more
general than in a beneficent Deity. The idea of a universal and beneficent Creator does not seem to arise in
the mind of man, until he has been elevated by long-continued culture.

MELVILLE

I was a good Christian; born and bred in the bosom of the infallible Presbyterian Church. How then
could I unite with this wild idolator in worshipping his
piece of wood? But what is worship? thought I. Do you
suppose now, Ishmael, that the magnanimous God of
heaven and earth— pagans and all included—can possibly be jealous of an insignificant bit of black wood?
Impossible! But what is worship?—to do the will of
God—*that* is worship. And what is the will of God?— to
do to my fellow man what I would have my fellow man
do to me—that is the will of God. Now, Queequeg is my
fellow man. And what do I wish that this Queequeg
would do to me? Why, unite with me in my particular
Presbyterian form of worship. Consequently, I must
then unite with him in his; ergo, I must turn idolator. So
I kindled the shavings; helped prop up the innocent little

idol; offered him burnt biscuit with Queequeg; salaamed before him twice or thrice; kissed his nose; and that done, we undressed and went to bed, at peace with our consciences and all the world. But we did not go to sleep without some little chat.

How it is I know not; but there is no place like a bed for confidential disclosures between friends. Man and wife, they say, there open the very bottom of their souls to each other; and some old couples often lie and chat over old times till nearly morning. Thus, then, in our hearts' honeymoon, lay I and Queequeg—a cosy, loving pair.

DARWIN

We can allow / satellites / planets / suns, universes, nay whole systems of universes to be governed by laws, but the smallest insect, we wish to be created at once by special act, provided with its instincts, its place in nature, its range...—must be a special act, or result of laws.... The Savage admires not a steam engine, but a piece of colored glass, is lost in astonishment at the artificer.—Our faculties are more fitted to recognize the wonderful structure of a beetle than a Universe.

MELVILLE

By the merest chance the ship itself at last rescued him; but from that hour the little negro went about the deck an idiot; such, at least, they said he was. The sea had jeeringly kept his finite body up, but drowned the infinite of his soul. Not drowned entirely, though. Rather carried down alive to wondrous depths, where strange shapes of the unwarped primal world glided to and fro before his passive eyes; and the miser-merman, Wisdom, revealed his hoarded heaps; and among the joyous, heartless, ever-juvenile eternities, Pip saw the multitudinous, God-omnipresent, coral insects, that out of the firmament of waters heaved the colossal orbs. He saw God's foot upon the treadle of the loom, and spoke it; and therefore his shipmates called him mad.

DARWIN

My F.[ather] says there is perfect gradation between sound people and insane.—that everybody is insane at some time.

MELVILLE

So man's insanity is heaven's sense; and wandering from all mortal reason, man comes at last to that celestial thought, which, to reason, is absurd and frantic; and weal or woe, feels then uncompromised, indifferent as his God.

DARWIN

—Have insane people any misgivings of the unjustness of their hatreds....—It must be so from the curious story of the Birmingham Doctor, praising his sister who confined him. & yet disinheriting her.—
...Doctor communicated to my grandfather his feeling of consciousness of insanity coming on—his struggles against it, his knowledge of the untruth of the idea, namely his poverty.—his manner of curing it by keeping the sum-total of his accounts in his pocket, & studying mathematics.

MELVILLE

Poor Hoffman—I remember the shock I had when I first saw the mention of his madness.—But he was just the man to go mad—imaginative, voluptuously inclined, poor, unemployed, in the race of life distanc[ed] by his inferiors, unmarried,—without a port or haven in the universe to make. His present misfortune—rather blessing—is but the sequel to a long experience of unwhole habits of thought.—This going mad of a friend or acquaintance comes straight home to every man who feels his soul in him,—which but few men do. For in all of us lodges the same fuel to light the same fire. And he who has never felt, momentarily, what madness is has but a mouthful of brains.

DARWIN

—My Father says after insanity is over people often think no more about it than of a dream.

MELVILLE

What sort of sensation permanent madness is may be very well imagined—just as we imagine how we felt when we were infants, tho' we can not recall it. In both conditions we are irresponsible & riot like gods without fear of fate.—It is the climax of a mad night of revelry when the blood has been transmuted into brandy.

DARWIN

(Case of Shrewsbury gentleman, unnatural union with turkey cock, was *restrained* by remonstrances on him.)... —Sometimes comes on suddenly from...

drinking cold drink.—then brain affected like getting suddenly into passion.—There seems no distinction between enthusiasm passion & madness.—ira furor brevis est. My father quite believes my grand F.[ather's] doctrine is true, that the only cure for madness is forgetfulness.

[PAUSE]

MELVILLE

The reason the mass of men fear God, and *at bottom dislike* Him, is because they rather distrust His heart, and fancy Him all brain like a watch. (You perceive I employ a capital initial in the pronoun referring to the Deity; don't you think there is a slight dash of flunkeyism in that usage?)

DARWIN

It is an argument for materialism, that cold water brings on suddenly in head, a frame of mind, analogous to those feelings, which may be considered as truly spiritual.

MELVILLE

Though in many of its aspects this visible world seems formed in love, the invisible spheres were formed in fright.

But not yet have we solved the incantation of...whiteness, and learned why it appeals with such power to the soul; and more strange and far more portentous—why, as we have seen, it is at once the most

meaning symbol of spiritual things, nay, the very veil of
the Christian's Deity; and yet should be as it is, the inten-
sifying agent in things the most appalling to mankind.

Is it that by its indefiniteness it shadows forth the
heartless voids and immensities of the universe, and
thus stabs us from behind with the thought of annihilation, when beholding the white depths of the milky way?
Or is it, that in essence whiteness is not so much a color
as the visible absence of color, and at the same time the
concrete of all colors; is it for these reasons that there is
such a dumb blankness, full of meaning, in a wide landscape of snows—a colorless, all-color atheism from
which we shrink?

DARWIN

I cannot pretend to throw the least light on such
abstruse problems. The mystery of the beginning of all
things is insoluble by us; and I for one must be content
to remain an Agnostic.

MELVILLE

Perhaps, after all, there is *no* secret. We incline to
think that the problem of the Universe is like the
Freemason's mighty secret, so terrible to all children. It
turns out, at last, to consist in a triangle, a mallet, and
an apron,—nothing more! We incline to think that God
cannot explain His own secrets, and that He would like
a little information on certain points Himself. We mor-
tals astonish Him as much as He us. But it is this *Being* of
the matter; there lies the knot with which we choke
ourselves. As soon as you say *Me*, a God, a *Nature*, so
soon you jump off from your stool and hang from the

beam. Yes, that word is the hangman. Take God out of the dictionary, and you would have him in the street.

DARWIN

Has the Creator since the Cambrian formation gone on creating animals with same general structure.—Miserable limited view.

MELVILLE

In reading some of Goethe's sayings, so worshipped by his votaries, I came across this, *"Live in the all."* That is to say, your separate identity is but a wretched one, —good; but get out of yourself, spread and expand yourself, and bring to yourself the tinglings of life that are felt in the flowers and the woods, that are felt in the planets Saturn and Venus, and the Fixed Stars. What nonsense! Here is a fellow with a raging toothache. "My dear boy," Goethe says to him, "you are sorely afflicted with that tooth; but you must *live in the all,* and then you will be happy!"

DARWIN

In the summer of 1818 I went to Dr. Butler's great school in Shrewsbury, and remained there for seven years till Midsummer 1825, when I was sixteen years old. I boarded at this school, so that I had the great advantage of living the life of a true schoolboy; but as the distance was hardly more than a mile to my home, I very often ran there in the longer intervals between the callings over and before locking up at night. This, I think, was in many ways advantageous to me by keeping up home affections and interests. I remember in the early part of my school life that I often had to run very quickly to be in time, and from being a fleet runner was generally successful; but when in doubt I prayed earnestly to God to help me, and I well remember that I attributed my success to the prayers and not to my quick running, and marvelled how generally I was aided.

MELVILLE

This "all" feeling, though, there is some truth in. You must often have felt it, lying on the grass on a warm summer's day. Your legs seem to send out shoots into the earth. Your hair feels like leaves upon your head. This is the *all* feeling. But what plays the mischief with the truth is that men will insist upon the universal application of a temporary feeling or opinion.

DARWIN

He who believes in the advancement of man from low organised form, will naturally ask how does this bear on the belief in the immortality of the soul. The barbarous races of man, as Sir J. Lubbock has shewn, possess no clear belief of this kind.

MELVILLE

It is a rainy morning; so I am indoors, and all work suspended. I feel cheerfully disposed, and therefore I write a little bluely. Would the Gin were here! If ever, my dear Hawthorne, in the eternal times that are to come, you and I shall sit down in Paradise, in some little shady corner by ourselves; and if we shall by any means be able to smuggle a basket of champagne there (I won't believe in a Temperance Heaven), and if we shall then cross our celestial legs in the celestial grass that is forever tropical, and strike our glasses and our heads together, till both musically ring in concert,— then, O my dear fellow-mortal, how shall we pleasantly discourse of all the things manifold which now so distress us,— when all the earth shall be but a reminiscence, yea, its final dissolution an antiquity. Then shall songs be composed as when wars are over: humorous, comic songs,—"Oh, when I lived in that queer little hole called the world," or, "Oh, when I toiled and sweated below," or, "Oh, when I knocked and was knocked in the fight"— yes, let us look forward to such things. Let us swear that, though now we sweat, yet it is because of the dry heat which is indispensable to the nourishment of the vine which is to bear the grapes that are to give us the champagne hereafter.

DARWIN

"The feeling of religious devotion is a highly complex one, consisting of love, complete submission to an exalted and mysterious superior, a strong sense of dependence, fear, reverence, gratitude, hope for the future, and perhaps other elements. No being could experience so complex an emotion until advanced in his intellectual and moral faculties to at least a moderately high level. Nevertheless, we see some distant approach to this state of mind in the deep love of a dog for his master, associated with complete submission, some fear, and perhaps other feelings."

MELVILLE

How nobly it rises our conceit of the mighty, misty

monster, to behold him solemnly sailing through a calm tropical sea; his vast, mild head overhung by a canopy of vapor, engendered by his incommunicable contemplations, and that vapor—as you will sometimes see it—glorified by a rainbow, as if Heaven itself had put its seal upon his thoughts. For, d'ye see, rainbows do not visit the clear air; they only irradiate vapor. And so, through all the thick mists of the dim doubts in my mind, divine intuitions now and then shoot, enkindling my fog with a heavenly ray. And for this I thank God; for all have doubts; many deny; but doubts or denials, few along with them, have intuitions. Doubts of all things earthly, and intuitions of some things heavenly; this combination makes neither believer nor infidel, but makes a man who regards them both with equal eye.

DARWIN

N.B. The explanation of types of structure in classes—as resulting from the *will* of the deity, to create animals on certain plans.—is no explanation—*it has not the character of a physical law* / & is therefore utterly useless. —it foretells nothing / because we know nothing of the will of the Deity, how it acts & whether constant or inconstant like that of man.—the cause given we know not the effect.

MELVILLE

We are to consider, that from the presumed great longevity of whales, their probably attaining the age of a century and more, therefore at any one period of time, several distinct adult generations must be contemporary. And what that is, we may soon gain some idea of, by imagining all the grave-yards, cemeteries, and family vaults of creation yielding up the live bodies of all the men, women, and children who were alive seventy-five years ago; and adding this countless host to the present human population of the globe.

DARWIN

Mac.[culloch] remarks all mammifers animals originally terrestrial.—for we find even in Cetaceæ traces of hind extremities.—How are we to explain this.—Did reptiles first inhabit seas.—Were they then killed out / by the intense cold /, & did mammifers then take their place? Would they not first occupy the Poles? Is this origin of the Polar attributes of the Cetaceæ,—How came Bats also? before birds? They are ancient.—Are Cetaceæ found in Paris Basin?

MELVILLE

"Dies, all dies!
The grass it dies, but in vernal rain
Up it springs and it lives again;
Over and over, again and again,
It lives, it dies and it lives again.
Who sighs that all dies?
Summer and winter, and pleasure and pain,
And everything everywhere in God's reign,
They end, and anon they begin again:
Wane and wax, wax and wane:
Over and over and over amain—
End, ever end, and begin again—
End, ever end, and forever and ever begin again!

DARWIN

Was witty in a dream in a confused manner.
Thought that a person was hung & came to life.

MELVILLE

Shall I send you a fin of the *Whale* by way of a specimen mouthful? The tail is not yet cooked —though the hell-fire in which the whole book is broiled might not unreasonably have cooked it all ere this. This is the book's motto (the secret one),—Ego non baptiso te in nomine—but make out the rest yourself.

DARWIN

I am aware that the conclusions arrived at in this work will be denounced by some as highly irreligious; but he who denounces them is bound to shew why it is more irreligious to explain the origin of man as a distinct species by descent from some lower form, through the laws of variation and natural selection, than to explain the birth of the individual through the laws of ordinary reproduction....

We thus learn that man is descended from a hairy, tailed quadruped, probably arboreal in its habits, and an inhabitant of the Old World. This creature, if its whole structure had been examined by a naturalist, would have been classed amongst the Quadrumana, as surely as the still more ancient progenitor of the Old and New World monkeys. The Quadrumana and all the higher mammals are probably derived from an ancient marsupial animal, and this through a long series of diversified forms, from some amphibian-like creature, and this again from some fish-like animal. In the dim obscurity of the past we can see that the early progenitor of all the Vertebrata must have been an aquatic animal provided with branchiæ, with the two sexes united in the same individual, and with the most important organs of the body (such as the brain and heart) imperfectly or not at all developed. This animal seems to have been more like the larvæ of the existing marine Ascidians than any other known form.

MELVILLE

Wherefore, for all these things, we account the whale immortal in his species, however perishable in his individuality. He swam the seas before the continents broke water; he once swam over the site of the Tuileries, and Windsor Castle, and the Kremlin. In Noah's flood he despised Noah's Ark; and if ever the world is to be again flooded, like the Netherlands, to kill off its rats, then the eternal whale will still survive, and rearing upon the topmost crest of the equatorial flood, spout his frothed defiance to the skies.

A Note on the Type

The principal text of *The Ape & The Whale* was
composed in a digitized version of Belwe Roman,
originally drawn in 1926 by Georg Belwe for the
Dresden typefoundry, Schelter & Giesecke. The
present version of Belwe has undergone a number
of revisions in the structure of individual letters
while still remaining faithful to the original
concepts of the designer.